PRINCETOWN

– ITS RISE AND PROGRESS –

by

William Crossing

QUAY
PUBLICATIONS
(BRIXHAM)

This is a limited edition
of 1000 copies
of which this book is

No. 210

November 1989

PRINCETOWN

– ITS RISE AND PROGRESS –

by

William Crossing

QUAY
PUBLICATIONS
(BRIXHAM)

ISBN 1 870083 30 X

Published by Quay Publications (Brixham)
P.O. Box 16, Brixham, Devon TQ5 8LW

Typeset by AJL Typesetting, Paignton, Devon TQ3 3HF

Printed in Great Britain
by Kingfisher Print & Design Limited
Dartington, Totnes, Devon TQ9 6TT

Acknowledgements

Acknowledgements for the photographs used in this publication are as follows: portrait of Sir Thomas Tyrwhitt, page 15, The Governing Body, Christ Church, Oxford, and also Lucy Whitaker, Assistant Curator of Pictures, for her kind assistance; Dartmoor War Prison, page 21, Devon County Library Services; John Swete's illustrations of Prince Hall and Two Bridges, volume 564M/F16, the Devon Records Office; and for the photographs and the postcards by Chapman & Son, Kingsway Road Photo Series, Valentine Series, W. E. Tooker and Weighell Publishers appearing on pages 38 and 58, Kath Brewer, Torquay; pages 53 (lower), 54, 57 (lower) and 61, David German, Princetown; pages 18 (lower), 32, 41 and 48, P. O. Joy, H.M. Prison Dartmoor, Princetown; pages 12, 18 (top), 29, 35, 42, 44, 50, 53 (top), 57 (top) 58 (top) and 60, Elisabeth Stanbrook, Brixham.

Front cover: An old plan of Dartmoor Prison and English Barracks and "A bit of Prince Town" from the *Illustrated London News*, 1st December, 1881.

INTRODUCTION

Had Thomas Tyrwhitt not been born, or if his circumstances had been different, Princetown would, in all probability, not exist, and William Crossing's series of articles entitled *Princetown – Its Rise and Progress* would not have appeared in the *Western Morning News* in 1906; written to commemorate the centenary of the laying of the prison's foundation stone.

William Crossing, born in Plymouth in 1847, was to become one of the leading authorities on Dartmoor, recording valuable social and topographical information for future generations.

Crossing's absorption with Dartmoor claimed most of his time – both that of his leisure and when he was supposed to be working. The latter contributed to the collapse of his father's mill at South Brent, and young Crossing's main source of income was then derived largely from writing plays for local theatres, series of Dartmoor articles for local newspapers and journals, and his books. His concern with recording social history brought him into contact with many moormen and people living in moorland towns and villages. Princetown was no exception and one of his acquaintances was Aaron Rowe, one time proprietor of the Duchy Hotel. It was his advice Crossing sought when he was searching for an illustrator for his *Guide to Dartmoor*. Rowe suggested a young man by the name of Philip Guy Stevens who was courting, and later married, his youngest daughter Beatrice in 1909.

Despite Crossing's success in the literary field, he died an ill and impoverished man and was buried with his wife Emma in Mary Tavy churchyard.

Although he died in 1928, he is still considered to be the most important author of Dartmoor literature, with many of his books still greatly sought.

This publication is the first time *Princetown – Its Rise and Progress* has appeared in book form and, where possible, old photographs have been used in keeping with a text which traces the history of this village from its beginnings in the late 1700s to the year when Crossing wrote the articles in 1906.

Thomas Tyrwhitt arrived on Dartmoor with the intention of taming and improving a vast tract of land he had leased from the Duchy of Cornwall, and creating a large agricultural estate using innovations in agricultural methods. With a high annual rainfall and a highly unsuitable terrain, it is not difficult to surmise why, despite shortlived success, this venture failed. Instead, Tyrwhitt revised his plans, and in 1806 the foundation stone of Dartmoor Prison was laid; a complex in which thousands of Napoleonic prisoners of war were to be confined.

Born in 1762, Thomas Tyrwhitt was a remarkable man who held many offices including Private Secretary to the Prince of Wales, M.P. for Okehampton and also for Plymouth, Auditor of the Duchy of Cornwall, Lord Warden of the Stannaries of Devon and Cornwall and, in 1812, he was knighted and made Gentleman Usher of the Black Rod. He died in France in 1833. A memorial tablet was erected in Princetown Church and is inscribed as follows:

SIR THOMAS TYRWHITT, KNT.
LATE OF TOR ROYAL
LORD WARDEN OF THE STANNARIES,
AND MANY YEARS USHER OF THE BLACK ROD.
DIED FEB. 24TH 1833
AGED 71.
HIS NAME AND MEMORY
ARE INSEPARABLE FROM ALL THE GREAT WORKS IN
DARTMOOR,
AND CANNOT CEASE TO BE HONOURED
IN THIS DISTRICT

Decorating the upper left and right hand corners of the tablet are the Tyrwhitt crest and the insignia and baton of the Order of the Garter.

Many changes have taken place in Princetown since Crossing wrote *Princetown – Its Rise and Progress* and, indeed, since his death in 1928. The Duchy Hotel was refurbished in 1908, the Railway Inn is now The Devil's Elbow, Bolt's Store has now passed out of the family and is known as the Corner Shop, pony and traps have been replaced by motor cars, North Hessary Tor has the adornment of a radio mast, the railway closed in 1956, Church Row or Government Row was pulled down and replaced with Woodville Terrace, Babb's Cottages were demolished too and replaced with Babb's Houses. The people with whom Crossing once conversed and from whom he undoubtedly obtained much of his information are now gone. Other changes have occurred too, with the coming and going of a variety of buildings, but one aspect that has remained constant throughout is the weather, with the village being able to boast one of the wettest areas in Britain.

Over 200 years have now elapsed since Thomas Tyrwhitt first cast his eyes over Dartmoor and chose the site for his proposed estate. It must have presented a bleak and desolate panorama, but the determination of this man never faltered. The setbacks and disappointments seemed to follow periods of prosperity which continued long after his death. Princetown is now firmly established on the map; a thriving community supporting a number of shops, cafés, public houses, places of worship, a garage, an information centre for the increasing number of tourists and, perhaps most important of all in view of the village's history, H.M. Prison Dartmoor. The survival of the prison has ensured the survival of the village around which it prospers.

Elisabeth Stanbrook
November 1989

CONTENTS

ILLUSTRATIONS

A FOREWORD

Nearly fourteen hundred feet above the sea, and in the midst of a desolate region where wild hills uplift their stony crusts, and rivers rise from turfy hollows, stands a little town, a modern Tadmor in the wilderness. Its years have yet been few, and some there are who dwell in it, or in the shadow of the tors that environ it, that have known those who remembered when on its site the heather and the ling bent to the breeze, and encumbering lumps of granite rose from the mass of waving bloom like grey islets in a purple ocean. But man intruded into Nature's fastness, wrestled with her, and compelled her to yield up some of her territory to him. Then gloomy walls arose, and the winds that swept from the fen changed their song of freedom to a mournful sigh as they passed over a place for captives. The grey isles were demolished, and man formed of them his dwellings; the heathery sea disappeared and fields took its place. The hamlet grew into a village; the village came to be regarded as a market town; and some there were who were gladdened that it was so. The years rolled on, and this little town in the wilds knew its alternating periods of depression and prosperity. And notwithstanding its remoteness from centres where men congregate its short history is not without interest, and perhaps there could be no more fitting time to glance at this than in the year that marks its centenary.

William Crossing

Siward's Cross, otherwise known as Nun's Cross, which forms one of the bond-marks between the Royal hunting-ground and the common of Walkhampton.

– Chapter One –

BEFORE THE DAWN

On the western side of the ancient Forest of Dartmoor an old stone cross, mentioned in a document of the 13th century, but which is probably of much earlier date, forms one of the bond-marks between the Royal hunting-ground and the common of Walkhampton. From this memorial of an olden day, which bears the name of Siward's Cross, the Forest boundary line runs northward along a ridge about the centre of which is a small tor called South Hisworthy, or, in local parlance, Hessary. Westward of the ridge are the commons; its eastern side is within the Forest, and here the ground slopes down to the Blackabrook and the Strane streams that find their way into the Dart. This slope is well sheltered from the westerly winds, the bane of Dartmoor, while towards the east it is protected to some extent by rising ground.

Towards the close of a day in the latter part of the 18th century two young men passed down this slope when on their way to their homes in the Forest. On nearing the foot of it they were somewhat surprised at seeing a heap of lime there, as, although ground had recently been enclosed in the vicinity they had not heard of any intention to erect buildings on the spot they had reached. But it was not long ere they learnt that one Mr. Thomas Tyrwhitt was about to build himself a residence on this pleasant slope, and to engage in agricultural operations on an extensive scale. The name of one of the young men was Cleave, and his ancestors had dwelt in the Forest during a considerable period. From his son, for many years my friend, and who now sleeps in the peaceful churchyard at Widecombe, I learnt this story. The work of which that heap of lime showed the commencement had far-reaching effects. Some may be disposed to regard these as beneficial, but true lovers of Nature who set a high value on this primeval region will be unable to share this view.

It was in 1785 when Mr Thomas Tyrwhitt, who was then 23 years of age, commenced his operations in the Forest, his attention in all probability having been directed to it in the performance of his duties as secretary to the Council of the Prince of Wales, his Royal Highness being the owner of the extensive waste. As mentioned in another place ("Hundred Years on Dartmoor") the district had been previously opened up by the formation of a road across it, the Act for which was obtained in 1772. A means of communication being thus provided, the Moor began to attract notice, and there were those who believed that it might be successfully cultivated, and that the poverty of soil and adverse climatic influences were difficulties that could be overcome. Tyrwhitt was one of these.

I have known several who remembered Tyrwhitt, and many more whose fathers recollected him in his early work, but I have never been able to gather any satisfactory account of the formation of the estate. In the 1826 edition of Carrington's "Dartmoor" some information on this point is given in a note, but unfortunately it is not very clear. It states that Tyrwhitt commenced his operations in 1785, and that Tor Royal, the name he gave to his estate, was "entirely formed by him in 1798, with his adjoining fields, plantations, and garden." By this we presume is meant that the work was completed in 1798, and thus extended over a period of thirteen years. But the actual date of the building of the house I cannot learn, though it seems probable that its erection, and the erection of some of the farm buildings, was one of the first things to be undertaken, and this we should naturally suppose would be the case. I have been told that a kind of huge garden vase formerly to be seen at Tor Royal bore the date 1785.

The road to which we have referred as having been commenced in 1772 ran from Tavistock across the Moor to Moretonhampstead. The present road over Dartmoor from the Rock, on Roborough Down, to Two Bridges, where it joins the former, was not made till some years later, so that when Tyrwhitt commenced to enclose his land the approach from the Down to that part of the Moor in which it was situated was by means of an ancient track, on the line from which the road was afterwards formed. From this track a narrow road was cut by Mr. Tyrwhitt as an approach to his house, and a lodge and a granite gateway were erected at the entrance to it on the common. This is known as Castle-road, and during late years has been taken over by the parish of Lydford. Mr. Tyrwhitt also made a road from this entrance to the Rundle Stone on the new Tavistock and Moreton road, which was about a mile and a half distant. There is good reason for believing that this, like the other roads on the Moor, was formed on the line of an old track. But the traffic over it must for many years have been less than that over the one which ran across Walkhampton Common to Roborough Down, small as that then was, and the old way was probably more in the nature of a green path than of a well-beaten track. This road,

Portrait Sir Thomas Tyrwhitt, founder of Dartmoor Prison and Princetown.

which was to become the main thoroughfare of a little town, shortened the distance between Tor Royal and Tavistock by about two miles.

Operations of the nature contemplated by Tyrwhitt would, of course, necessitate the employment of a number of persons, and for some of these accommodation would have to be found near the scene of their labours. An inn was accordingly built not far from the entrance gate, and by the side of the track that ran over the common. It was called the Plume of Feathers, in allusion to the ostrich feather badge of the Prince of Wales, and is still standing. Whether Tyrwhitt was the builder of this house is not quite certain, but there is reason for supposing such to be the case. However this may be, we shall hardly be wrong in accepting the statement that has been handed down in the neighbourhood from father to son, and which goes to show that this inn is about a hundred and twenty years old; this would point to it having been erected at the time the operations at Tor Royal were commenced. Probably a few of the cottages in the Plymouth road were also built in the early days of Tor Royal, but some years subsequently to the erection of the Plume of Feathers.

According to another note in the editions of Carrington already referred to, Tyrwhitt's estate extended over 2,000 acres, held under lease from the Duchy of Cornwall. It included a large tract of land now known as Tor Royal Newtake, the enclosing of which deprived the venville tenants of much good pasturage, the statement made in the above-named work that Tyrwhitt's operations were conducted " on the very worst part of the Forest" being altogether erroneous. But the welfare of the men to whom the Moor was valuable as a vast cattle and sheep run was a consideration that appears to have weighed very lightly with those who believed they could profitably reclaim it. So long as the Duchy was willing to grant leases they were ready to take them, and seem to have entirely ignored the rights of others. By the formation of large enclosures they not only took from the venville tenant and the holders of the ancient Forest tenements much good grazing ground, but caused great inconvenience as well. The walls of their newtakes stretch from one side of the Forest to the other, thus cutting off the southern part of the Moor from the northern.

The site chosen by Mr. Tyrwhitt for his residence was about 1,300 feet above sea level. The house was substantially built, and low, as a Dartmoor dwelling should be. It consists of a central portion of one storey, and attics with dormer windows, and two extensive wings with a ground floor only. It is well calculated to withstand the storms of winter, but during its first years had only the South Hisworthy ridge to shield it from the western blasts. In time however, an additional shelter was afforded by the plantations so judiciously formed by the enterprising agriculturist who attempted with such pertinacity to tame the Moor. In addition to the lodge at the gate on the Moor track near the Plume of Feathers there was another at the entrance to the grounds surrounding the house. There were excellent outbuildings and a walled garden; the latter is not now cultivated, but I believe much excellent fruit has been grown there.

But although Tyrwhitt took so deep an interest in his Dartmoor venture, expending large sums of money in his efforts to subdue the waste, he was only able to pass part of his time at Tor Royal, his duties calling him away from the Westcountry. He filled many important offices besides that of secretary to the Prince of Wales. In 1786 he was appointed auditor of the Duchy. Ten years later he was elected member of Parliament for Okehampton, which place he represented till 1802; in 1805 he was appointed Lord Warden of the Stannaries, and in the following year again went to Parliament as member for Plymouth, and later became Gentleman-Usher of the Black Rod, when he was knighted.

With the lapse of time the tales once current of the early days of Tor Royal are dropping out of men's memories. They spoke of the jovial gatherings there when Tyrwhitt would come down from London to visit his Forest farm, glad no doubt to exchange for a time the atmosphere in which he lived for the freedom of the Moor. Then would he extend his hospitality to his friends, and, as the old Forest dwellers were wont to tell, there were glorious times at Tor Royal. Those were the days of two, or even three, bottle men, when guests sat long at tables, and had often to be helped to bed. Then would the ancient son of Dartmoor open his eyes in wonder on learning how gentlemen enjoyed themselves. Aye, and open them wider still when he discovered that it was not the Moor only that proved an attraction for them. If old gossips spoke truly, the young master of Tor Royal and his guests found as much delight in gazing upon the cherry cheeks and bright eyes of the rustic beauties of the neighbourhood as they did in acquainting themselves with the agricultural capabilities of the great waste.

And so the years went on, and although Tyrwhitt, according to report, may have shown himself a believer in the old adage and indulged occasionally in what we are told is a preventative to dullness, nothing is more certain than that he devoted himself earnestly to all that he undertook. That which he has left upon Dartmoor is sufficient to show us that his labours there were unceasing, and that if perseverance could have ensured success he would have proved the victor in his battle with Nature. He erected several small dwellings on the land which he had set his heart upon seeing yield to the cultivator. In addition to the two lodges previously mentioned he built a cottage at South Hisworthy Tor for a labourer on the estate named Symons. It is no longer in existence, but its foundations may be traced; they are close

Tor Royal, once the residence of Thomas Tyrwhitt.

A rare photograph of the old Tor Royal Lodge.

to the tor, and on its eastern side. An old lady living in the neighbourhood, who is now 87 years of age, remembers it very well, having visited it many times. Southward of this, and by the side of the road that now leads to Whiteworks, at a point known as Castle Gate, Tyrwhitt built another, but, like the former, it has disappeared. Still further south another was erected, and this, which is now in the occupation of Mr. William Worth, was the forerunner of the little hamlet of Peat Cot, which at present consists of four cottages. Tyrwhitt also built Swincombe at the eastern end of his great newtake, as well as Bull Park, which is situated at no great distance from the house. The erection of another dwelling is also attributed to him. This is The Ockery, which stands on the bank of the Blackabrook, and is noticed further on.

Although no conspicuous success attended the labours of Tyrwhitt, nor those of his fellow venturers at Two Bridges and Prince Hall, he was still, after a trial of twenty years, full of hope. He continued in his endeavour to point the way, but few there were who followed him; there was no responsive echo to his call. The road across the Forest was comparatively untravelled, the Plume of Feathers depended for its custom upon a few labourers and passing drivers of pack-horses. The face of the Moor was altered somewhat, it is true, from what it was when he first set to work to build his walls, but its frown had nevertheless not yet changed to a smile. The time when men should gather upon it, and the "hum of industry" be heard, still seemed far off. But it was the lull before the storm; the course of events was about to change.

England being at that time at war with France large numbers of the foe were brought as prisoners to our shores. The depot at Plymouth, and the prison ships, were inconveniently crowded, and more adequate and healthier accommodation was urgently needed. It occurred to Tyrwhitt that Dartmoor offered itself as a suitable place on which to build a war prison, and representations to this effect were made to the Government. An official of the Transport Board was sent down to meet Mr. Daniel Alexander, the architect, and after examining many places on the Moor they fixed on a spot under North Hisworthy Tor as fitting for the purpose. This was near the scene of Tyrwhitt's operations, and in all probability was suggested by him. The building was ordered to be erected, and plans were prepared. On the 20th March, 1806, Mr. Tyrwhitt laid the foundation-stone, and with it was laid the foundation of Princetown.

✣ ✣ ✣

– Chapter Two –

DAYBREAK

The spot on which it was designed to erect the great war prison, though remote, was easily accessible from Plymouth, a good road having been made many years previously from the Tavistock highway on Roborough Down to Two Bridges. This followed the line of the old track over Walkhampton Common before referred to, and was the work of Mr. Heywood, of Maristowe. The hamlet which the prison called into existence sprang up on this road; the Plume of Feathers, the two or three cottages near it, Mr. Tyrwhitt's lodge, and probably the house now known as the Railway Inn, which, however, was subsequently enlarged, and a toll-house, forming its nucleus. The site chosen for the prison was close to the road made by Mr. Tyrwhitt from his lodge to the Rundle Stone, and this being afterwards improved and rendered suitable, there was a good approach to it both from the Plymouth and the Tavistock road. As I have elsewhere stated ("Hundred Years on Dartmoor") a gate was placed at each end of it; one just opposite to the Plume of Feathers (the granite posts may still be seen near by), and the other not far to the east of Rundle Stone Corner, and a short distance from the house at present existing there. This road, though still continuing to be a thoroughfare, was thus under the control of the prison authorities.

The author of the notes to the edition of Risdon's "Survey of the County of Devon," issued in 1811, has given a very good description of the prison, which is particularly valuable in having been written just after the building was completed. In addition to this, it is figured in Vancouver's "General View of the Agriculture of the County of Devon," which was published in 1808, and this agrees with the description given in the book named. An old coloured bird's-eye view of it also exists, and between this and the illustration in Vancouver there are no essential points of difference. The surroundings of the prison in the latter are altogether fanciful; in the coloured view, which is taken from another side of the building, and is much in the nature of a plan, no surroundings are shown, but in addition

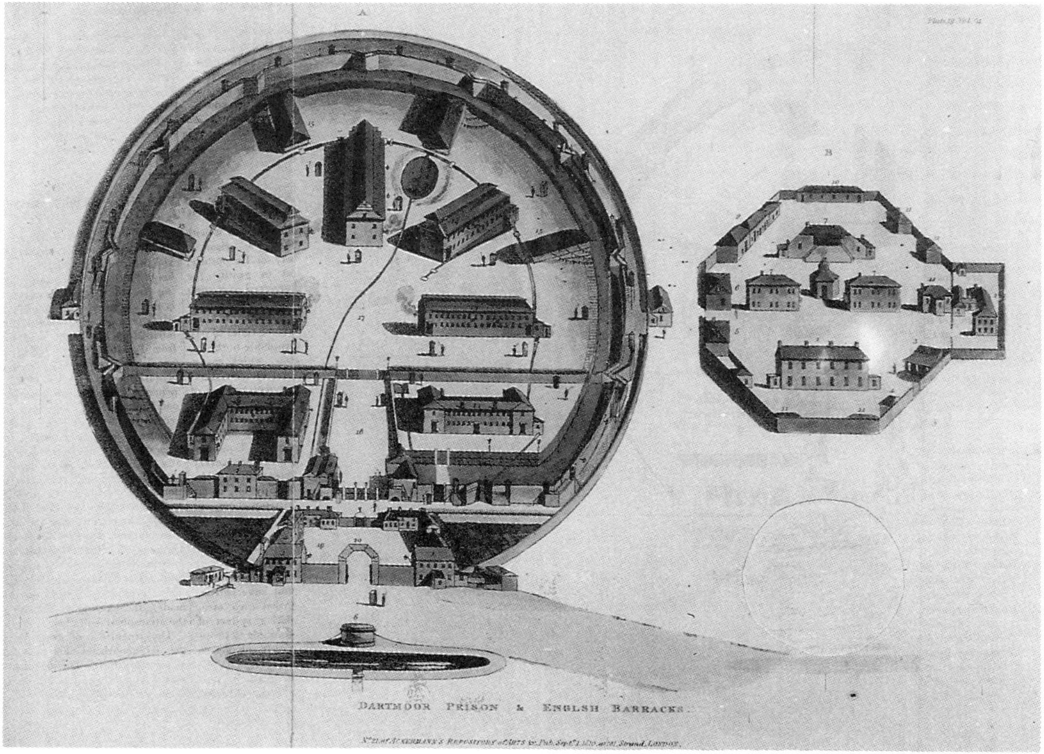

An old plan of Dartmoor Prison and English Barracks.

to the prison the barracks erected for the troops forming the guard over the prisoners are represented. In the notes to Carrington's "Dartmoor" there is also an account of the building. This gives some further particulars, and is, consequently, of value, but does not perhaps possess quite so great an interest as the contemporary description in Risdon. These notices and illustrations enable us to form a good idea of the appearance of

"that proud pile where England held
Within her victor-grip her vanquish'd foe."

The land required for the purposes of the prison was about 390 acres, and a lease of this was granted by the Duchy for a term of ninety-nine years. The prison itself occupied a circular space of about thirty acres, which was surrounded by a lofty wall, the same that forms the boundary of the present convict prison; this area was half a mile in circumference. Within this wall was another, the space between the two forming a wide military road. Here the guard paraded, and sentinels were posted on platforms built against the inner wall, from which they could overlook the whole of the prison. It used to be said that the watchword took a quarter of an hour in passing round. At one time bells were fixed on the outer wall, so that a prisoner attempting to scale it would immediately sound an alarm. The inner enclosure, in which the prisoners were confined, did not form a complete circle, a segment being cut off from it on the western side, or that near the entrance. The outer gateway is still standing, and exhibits a style of architecture singularly appropriate to the material of which it is built, but the motto – "Parcere Subjectis" – graven on its granite is no longer so. On each side of the gateway was a residence, one being appropriated to the governor, and the other to the surgeon. A short distance within this entrance, from which the ground sloped, was another gate, formed in a wall that ran entirely across and joined the outer circular wall on either side. In the space thus cut off there were dwellings and offices, and in the coloured view plots of grass are also represented. Inside the second gate was another space, across which ran the military road, and on the further side of it, in a direct line with the other two, was a third entrance, having folding gates. This was placed in the inner wall, or barrier, which was formed partly of buildings, and gave admission to that part of the establishment in which the prisoners were confined. This was sub-divided by a barrier of masonry surmounted with iron palisades. In the part first reached there were two large buildings, standing in enclosures, one on each hand. Of these one was a hospital, the other being appropriated to petty officers, who were separated from the men. Beyond the barrier, and in a space considerably larger than that occupied by the remainder of the great prison, and which was of a semi-circular form, stood the great buildings in which the men were confined, each of which was capable of containing over 1,500 prisoners. When the prison was opened there were five of these, but according to Mr William Burt, secretary of the Plymouth Chamber of Commerce in 1826, the number was afterwards increased to seven, the two additional buildings being erected by the prisoners. On the completion of these, there was accommodation for 9,600 men, or even more. The buildings were each 300 feet long and 50 feet wide, and were arranged on one general plan. There were two floors, in which a double tier of hammocks were slung on cast-iron pillars, and there was a third floor in the roof, which was used as a promenade during the inclement weather. Sheds were also provided for a similar purpose in the exercise ground, and these, as the views show, were placed between the larger buildings. The prisoners were prevented from approaching the inner wall enclosing the area over which they were permitted to roam by high railings, and the coloured view represents the ground between these and this wall as being covered with turf.

On the south side of the prison were the barracks, the wall of which enclosed a space octagonal in shape. Here there was accommodation for eighteen officers and four hundred and eighty-four non-commissioned officers and privates, a force deemed sufficiently strong to guard the prisoners.

The building of the great prison and barracks, which was carried out under the superintendence of Mr Daniel Alexander, the architect, at an original cost of about £130,000, it is almost unnecessary to say, afforded work for a large number of men. As these in most cases came from a distance dwellings had to be provided for them, and these being erected near the Plume of Feathers, the once lonely wayside inn soon found itself the centre of a hamlet. It speedily had a rival, too. This was the house near to it, now called the Railway Inn, and which was enlarged about that time, as previously mentioned. A small beginning this, but the plant was to grow and become a tree. The day had broken, and though clouds were to pass across the sky, they were to hide only for a time the sun of hope.

The building of the prison proceeded rapidly, and in December 1808, it was ready for the reception of the unhappy men, whose only crime was that they had fought for their country. Whether the selection of such a spot for their incarceration was wise is not perhaps to be decided at this distance of time, but it is certainly difficult to understand why it was deemed necessary to immure prisoners of war in such a desolate region, and thus permit their sufferings to be added to by the dreariness of their surroundings. But, as we have already seen, it was Tyrwhitt who suggested the Moor as being suitable for such a purpose, and there can be little doubt that this desire to draw attention to it influenced him in a great measure. He was very sanguine as to the capabilities of Dartmoor, and believed that if once it was opened up settlers would be attracted to it. Naturally, too, his connection with the Duchy inspired him with a wish to turn the great tract of land forming part of its possessions to more profitable account, and that such was possible he had endeavoured to show by his experiments at Tor Royal. Government works on Dartmoor would bring people to it, and thus one of his chief points would be gained. That he honestly believed the Moor to be well adapted for such a purpose as he recommended no one will doubt. At the same time, it is probable that had he not been in some measure a visionary it would never have been selected.

Although the prison was not opened until 1809, buildings of some kind were completed within twelve months of the laying of the foundation-stone, as is proved by the baptismal register. On the first page of this is the following:–

"Register of Baptisms at the Prison of War, Dartmoor, within the parish of Lidford (sic), where Divine service has been performed from January 25th, 1807, under the sanction of the Bishop of the Diocese, by James Holman Mason, M.A., Vicar of Treneglos and Warbstow."

The first entry in the register is of the date April 12th in the same year.

"Henry, son of Richard Badcock and Martha his wife, living at Prince Hall: received his full baptism."

It is probable that the baptismal rites, in most cases at least, were at this time performed at the houses of the parents, the word "privately" being frequently added to the entries. The Rev. J. H. Mason afterwards became vicar of Widecombe-in-the-Moor.

While the prison and barracks were in course of erection it is probable that other buildings were also constructed. Bakehouses, and slaughter-houses were built, it was said by the contractors who supplied the commissariat department at the prison, and it is most likely that these were completed at the same time as the latter. One of the bakeries occupied the site of the present Roman Catholic priest's house, and another stood on the spot where Emmanuel Angel, the sexton, now lives. This was a large one, with a number of ovens. Richard Edwards, of Whiteworks, who died about thirty years ago, aged 98, used to work there as a baker, and he was also employed at Tor Royal. The slaughter-houses, or Butchery, as the buildings were formerly termed, stood on the site of the present schools. A little later a brewery was established. This was situated inside the Barrack Gate, as the one opposite to the Plume of Feathers was called, and now forms the kitchen of the Duchy Hotel. A large copper vat is to be seen in the yard at the rear. This hotel was originally built for officers' quarters, but whether at the same time as the brewery is not certain. It dates, however, from the early days of the prison. There was also a corn mill from which the bakeries were supplied with flour, but this may not have been built until after the opening of the prison. It was situated near Bachelor's Hall, where a mine had been worked only a few years previously, and near it, and between the present Bachelor's Hall Farm and the Blackabrook, were four or five cottages, erected in all probability for the workmen. The mill and cottages have now disappeared, but wheel pits are still to be seen there, and until recently one of the stones used for grinding.

With the arrival of the prisoners and their guards in 1809 there was a further change in the hamlet that had grown up around the Plume of Feathers. The place that had already worn a busy look during the three years necessary for the work of preparing for the reception of so large a body of men, now became the scene of much greater animation as the people entered on the task of providing for their wants. More houses were added to it, and by-and-bye, when a church was built, it had all the features of a little town.

– Chapter Three –

LIGHT WITHOUT : GLOOM WITHIN

In one of his notes to Carrington's poem Mr. William Burt, after briefly describing the prison, which had then – 1826 – been closed for several years, observes that the natural result of such an establishment was the gradual formation of a small town, and this, he says, was called Princetown, in honour of the Prince of Wales, who when Mr. Burt wrote had succeeded to the Throne. But I am not at all sure that the name had originally any connection with the Prince. It was heard on Dartmoor before the foundation-stone of the prison was laid; indeed, it is on record that it was applied to a place in the locality ten years previous to that event. There is reason for believing that Two Bridges, a mile and a half distance, was sometimes known as Princetown, and I am disposed to think that the name may been been derived from the ancient tenement of Prince Hall near by, which is mentioned in early records of the Forest. Two Bridges, although not shown on the plan of the road, or track, over Dartmoor in Owen's " Britannia Depicta," published in 1620, existed long before the close of the 18th century. In 1770 a market for potatoes was held there, that year being remarkable for the fine crops grown in the neighbourhood of Moretonhampstead; they were brought to this central part of the Moor, where they were purchased for disposal in Plymouth. Two Bridges is also mentioned by name in the Act of 1772, passed for making the road over Dartmoor. In 1780 a Mr. Gullet, one of the earliest of those who formed the idea that boggy and rocky land could be made to produce crops at a profit, commenced his experiments at Prince Hall, and the estate was afterwards acquired by Judge Buller. It is not improbable that when this old Forest farm was in the possession of the latter its name may have become attached to Two Bridges. In many parts of Devon, and particularly in the Dartmoor parishes, the word "town" signifies no more than one farmhouse, so that even if Two Bridges consisted of only a single dwelling the term would be applicable. But Judge Buller not only greatly improved the house at Prince Hall, but

Prince Hall situated near the West Dart river, in 1797. From a watercolour by John Swete.

Two Bridges in 1797, with the Saracen's Head Inn. From a watercolour by John Swete.

also built some cottages and an inn at Two Bridges, the sign of which, the Saracen's Head, had reference to his crest, so that quite a little settlement was formed there by him. Whether there was a toll-gate there at that time I cannot discover; the earliest reference to one that I can find is in 1816. Judge Buller also enclosed much land, and took considerable interest in the welfare of his labourers, and of those who dwelt round him. The little hostelry and the two or three cottages near it might very well have been referred to as the "town", and having such a close connection with Prince Hall, might sometimes have been spoken of as Princetown. That it was so seems to be proved by an account of a visit to Dartmoor in 1796 by Mr. Arthur Young, an authority on agriculture. Among other places inspected by him was Two Bridges which he refers to as Princetown and from there he went to Prince Hall.

Young speaks in highly eulogistic terms of Judge Buller's attempts to cultivate the Moor and it is evident that he, in common with other agriculturists of his time, thought there was wisdom in trying to accomplish it, ignoring the fact of its already possessing considerable value as a grazing ground for cattle, sheep and ponies. He speaks of it as "these deserts," and as though it were entirely unproductive, which perhaps is hardly to be wondered at, seeing that he knew very little about it. After saying that the result of Judge Buller's work ought to open the eyes of the country to its capabilities, he tells us that "Dartmoor at present is a disgrace to the kingdom – it might be what Princetown is, a garden."

We are not here concerned with the opinion of Mr. Young, nor with the fact that Dartmoor, in spite of the attempts made to subdue it, is no more like a garden now than it was a hundred and ten years ago, but merely with this early mention of Princetown and its application to Two Bridges. At the time of Mr. Young's visit Mr. Edward Bray, of Tavistock, had for some years been engaged in agricultural operations at Bear Down, which is close to Two Bridges, and the spot being a sheltered one the trees that he planted there throve exceedingly well, and we can therefore understand Mr. Young's remark, though we may not agree with it. But it is certain there was nothing near the Plume of Feathers to warrant it, and consequently he could not have had that spot in his mind. We are thus forced to one of two conclusions – either that Two Bridges was sometimes called Princetown, or that Young made a mistake. Seeing that the companions of his trip may be supposed to have known something about the Moor, it is not easy to imagine the latter.

Mr. J. Brooking Rowe, in a most interesting account of Tyrwhitt's life and work, gives an extract from the "Bristol Mirror" of the 18th July, 1805, in which it is stated that the Prince of Wales was about to erect at his own

Bear Down Farm, once the residence of Mr Edward Bray. Services used to be held here.

expense a chapel at Princetown in the Forest of Dartmoor; and also that Mr. Tyrwhitt had suggested the propriety of erecting a war prison near that place. This certainly may have had reference to the Plume of Feathers and the few cottages near it, though such a description of the site would be sufficiently correct had Two Bridges been intended. Religious services had already been held near the last-named spot, by Judge Buller at Prince Hall, and by Mr. Bray at Bear Down; and the need of a regular place of worship there might have become apparent. Two Bridges was far more central than the Plume of Feathers, and a chapel there would have served the needs of the Forest tenants; but if it ever was the intention of the Prince to build one on the Moor such was never carried out. If, however, we suppose that by 1805 the inn near his lodge, the toll-house, and the cottages by the roadside, had received the name of Princetown, as being appropriate to the settlement then likely to arise in the Forest, of which the Prince of Wales was lord, it is still a question whether it was not previously borne by Two Bridges.

But whatever view we may take of this, it is certain that it was some time before the name came into general use. In a letter written in 1805 by an official of the Transport Board relative to the proposed site of the prison no mention is made of Princetown, but the spot is spoken of as being near to Mr. Tyrwhitt's lodges. In 1808 Vancouver's book appeared, containing the drawings of the prison before alluded to, but Princetown is not named in it; in 1809 Warner published his "Tour Through Cornwall," in which is an account of a short stay that he made at Ashburton in the previous year, and in this he speaks of Tyrwhitt's work on the Moor, but there is no reference whatever to Princetown. Two years later, that is in 1811, the edition of Risdon with notes bringing it down to date was issued. The notice of Dartmoor occupies several pages; the labours of Judge Buller and Tyrwhitt and others are referred to, there is a description of the prison, as already stated, and mention is made of the settlement near it, but the name of Princetown does not occur. Neither is it shown on Ebden's map of Devon, nor on Cary's, both of which were published in 1811. On Ebden's map three objects are marked– the "Prison," "Barracks," and "Lodge," the latter being the one at the entrance to Mr. Tyrwhitt's drive; on Cary's map the words "New Prison" appear. It is not until 1812 that I can find the place indisputably referred to as Princetown. In that year the following entry occurs in the baptismal register:–

"October 4. Ann, daughter of William Robins and Ann his wife, resident at Prince Town Brewery."

After 1815 the name often appears in the register, but notwithstanding this there is evidence, as we shall see later on, that it was not widely known.

While the years following 1808 were full of activity in the little town that had so suddenly sprung into being, and men's hopes concerning it were high in the flush of the coming day, within the grim walls under Hisworthy there was much of gloom and sorrow. Gleams of merriment there may have been, for many of the prisoners were careless, and though deprived of that without which life loses all its sweetness, indulged in dance and song. But there were others to whom their captivity was irksome, and hardly to be borne, and whose thoughts were ever turned to their homes beyond the sea. Outside their prison was a land dreary to look upon when the clouds rested on its pinnacles of granite, but it was at least a land of freedom. And, moreover, it did not always frown, for when the sun chased the mists away the ancient hills, uplifting themselves into warmth and light, lost their forbidding aspect. But within the great circle of masonry the gloom ever attendant on captivity rested like a pall. The song and the jest might serve to pass the idle hours, but even the thoughtless must have had heavy hearts sometimes, when penned within their prison in a land of strangers they remembered how uncertain was the day of liberty.

Originally erected for the reception of French prisoners of war, the great building on the Moor was destined to receive men of many nations. There were Danes who had been compelled to fight on the side of Napoleon; Malays, Eurasians, and even Chinese, taken from Dutch vessels; and later, Americans, including a large number of negroes, the latter, it is said, being separated from the others. Escapes were very frequent, and during the time the Americans were there an attempt was made to tunnel under walls, and would probably have succeeded had not one of the prisoners betrayed his comrades. It is rather surprising to learn that men in such a condition were able to manufacture a base coin, but they contrived to obtain a supply of metal for that purpose, and also procured Spanish silver dollars, from each of which they made eight English shillings. They also forged Bank of England notes, as well as notes on local banks to the extent of several thousand pounds. Some of the guard acted as confederates in passing these and being discovered were transported for the offence. Much of this money was also passed in the market, held daily in that part of the prison nearer to the outer entrance gate, and to which produce was brought from Tavistock, Chagford, Moretonhampstead, and other places in the neighbourhood. Those of the prisoners who were more honestly inclined obtained money by the manufacture of various useful and ornamental articles, which they sold to the market people, and by these means were able to purchase poultry and vegetables, and such like, and so supplement their meagre rations.

Thus during the day there was a busy scene within the prison, and in

A ship made from bones and human hair by a French prisoner of war.

the street of the little town, where people were constantly arriving and departing. At night, when the Moor lay under a darkened sky, the captives looked from their barred windows upon murky gloom, faintly illuminated by the dim light of the lamps fixed at the corners of the buildings, and on the walls, that the sentinels posted on the platforms might watch the prison-houses. But the rays, though dull, were yet brighter than the hopes of many behind the gratings.

✣ ✣ ✣

– Chapter Four –

EARLY MORN

It is probable that the Dartmoor man viewed the settlement planted in his midst with very little surprise or curiosity. He had already witnessed several attempts to win wealth from the waste (none of which, by the way, could be said to have proved a success) and a further venture, though in another direction, would hardly be a matter for wonder. Besides he is by no means given to pry into matters that do not concern him, and it is very likely that he regarded the building of the prison, and the formation of the town near it, with apathy, only interesting himself in the fact that the former provided a market near at home for a portion of his produce. At the same time the place would have a certain attraction for him. To many of the Moorland dwellers the sight of a multitude was rare; that of a busy street, one almost unknown, and therefore we can well believe that, for a time at least, their visits to it were frequent, and that it often formed the topic of their conversation.

The baptismal register affords us a glimpse of the busy times of the war prison, since we learn from it the callings of many then living in Princetown. Mention has already been made of William Robins, who resided at the brewery in 1812. In 1814 we find that others connected with it were Thomas Bennett and Robert Roddon, the former being described as a yeoman resident at the brewery, and the latter as a labourer lately working there. We have also mention of John Arnold, a steward, and of William Gover, a framework knitter, of Ottery St. Mary, both of whom were employed at the prison; and of George Challacombe, who is named as the carter at that establishment. We can find also bakers, butchers, millers, blacksmiths and canal men, the latter no doubt being responsible for the maintenance of the leat by means of which the prison was supplied with water. This leat, which terminates at a reservoir opposite to the prison gateway, is about four miles in length, and is fed from an affluent of the Walkham called Spriddle Lake, but water can also be taken from the first-named stream if required. One of these men, Thomas Chapman, in 1809, lived in a hut near the prison; the name of another, Peter Sermon, occurs in the register six years later.

Among the militia forming the guard, or part of the guard, over the prisoners, are the names of John Chapple, stonemason, of Southmolton, sergeant-major in the South Devon; John Chaloner, cordwainer, also of the South Devon; James Massey, sergeant in the Royal Cheshire; Thomas Ross, of Dingwald, in Ross-shire, private in the Royal Lancashire; and George Spear, private in the Monaghan.

Others named in the register, and apparently not connected with the prison, include yeomen, husbandmen, labourers, miners, innkeepers, and turnpikemen. The miners were probably employed at Whiteworks, as according to information supplied by Mr. J. Taylor to Lysons, for the latter's Devonshire volume of "Magna Britannia," Bachelor's Hall Mine had ceased working in 1810. After the appearance of Lysons' book, however, which was in 1822, this mine was restarted, and is noticed hereafter. Two other mines, Nuns and Keaglesbarrow, both in the vicinity of Princetown, were also abandoned previous to 1810.

John Ellis is mentioned as an innkeeper in Princetown in 1815, and Edward Worth as also keeping an inn there in 1816. There is nothing to show whether this points to one or to two inns, but there were at that time two in the village, the Plume of Feathers and the one afterwards called the Railway Inn. The occupier of the former in 1850 was John Leger, and about twenty-eight years later the lease was handed over to the Duchy by Mrs. Leger, the property having fallen into a dilapidated state; it was then taken by Mr. Crocker, father of the present landlord. In the same year (1850) the Railway Inn was in the possession of the Princetown worthy presently noticed.

There was also an inn near the northern end of the road made by Mr. Tyrwhitt. The house still exists, but has been much improved by convict labour, and is the one to which the boundary gate before mentioned was near. It was called the Rundle Stone Inn, and continued to be a house of entertainment until about 1854, when also the gates were removed. This house was at one time kept by a landlord named Hannaford, whose descendants are still living in the neighbourhood. The name of the last landlord was Friend. Another inn stood by the roadside near the Cherry Brook.

The tollhouse at Princetown was known as the Roundhouse, and was situated opposite to the Plume of Feathers, and a short distance in front of the present Duchy Hotel. When the houses were built on the Plymouth road, which would be about the time that the prison was opened (though

The Plume of Feathers, the oldest inn in Princetown. The proprietor's name above the door is J. Crocker. Note the Jubilee Lamp on the left which was erected by public subscription in 1887.

Plymouth Road showing houses that were later demolished and replaced with others set further back from the road. The New London houses are on the skyline.

those bearing the name of Babb's Cottages were not erected until about 1853), there was also a turnpike gate at the entrance to the village in that direction, but the tolls were always taken at the Roundhouse. In 1817 William Osmond, who is described as a miller, was living at the house, and subsequently the gates were for many years in charge of a Mrs Lee who is still remembered by two or three of the older inhabitants. In later years, when the tolls were abolished, John Luggard, an ostler at the Duchy Hotel, lived in the old house; the last to occupy it was John Wills, also an ostler at the same hotel. Other turnpikes in the neighbourhood were at Two Bridges, already mentioned, and at Cherry Brook.

Many now living at Princetown are descended from those who witnessed its birth, knew it in the morning of its days, enjoyed its prosperity, and saw its decline. Among these may be named James Rowe, grandfather of the present well-known host of the Duchy Hotel, Mr. Aaron Rowe. If there were many men of his stamp in the little town it is not a matter for wonder that it made such rapid strides. Able to turn his hand almost to anything, he was just the man that was wanted in the new settlement. In 1815 his name occurs in the register, where he is described as a master blacksmith, residing at Princetown. The worker in iron is of all individuals one of the most useful, but James Rowe was very much more than that. At one time he was the landlord of the Railway Inn, which he was still occupying in 1850; in the early days he kept a store in the same house, where those who preferred " the cups that cheer, but not inebriate" were able to purchase tea; the housewife desirous of baking bread or pickling pork could obtain from him her flour and salt, and also be supplied with many other articles of daily use. And while man's necessities were thus catered for, the alleviation of one of the most distressing ills that he is heir to also claimed James Rowe's attention. He added to his other accomplishments a knowledge of dentistry. The instruments he used were no doubt very effective; they are still in existence, and in appearance are suggestive of the torture chamber of the Tower of London or the Spanish Inquisition. There was much of the philanthropist about James Rowe; his dentistry did not always bring him gain. Not being able to witness unmoved the dreadful state to which his patients were sometimes reduced after one of his operations, it was his custom to offer them refreshments in the shape of hot spirit and water, and as his fee for extracting a tooth was sixpence, and the refreshment cost him the same, it is obvious that he often exercised his skill with no profit. A few years before he died James Rowe handed over his "practice" to his son, James Julian Rowe, father of the present Mr. Aaron Rowe.

There are now living in or near Princetown three daughters of Richard Edwards, who, as we have previously stated, was a baker there during the time of the war prison. They are all widows, the eldest being Charlotte Worth, of Peat Cot, and mother of the little colony there. She is not however, exactly its founder, as the cottage from which the hamlet took its name , and another nearby, were standing before her time. These have already been alluded to. The former was occupied in 1809 by a labourer named John Widden; the latter which was known as South Castle, and stood on the spot now called Castle Gate, was in 1811 in the occupation of Henry Marks, a miner, who was probably employed at Whiteworks. Charlotte Worth attained the age of 94 in January last; she was baptised at Princetown on 2nd April 1815. Two sisters, Mrs Mortimer and Mrs Hill, the former 87, and the latter 81 years of age, live in Princetown; another sister, Mrs Sergeant, aged 78, recently left the neighbourhood, to go to reside with a daughter at Nottingham. A photograph of the four sisters was taken at Princetown about two years ago. An enthusiast describes them as being young and active. Well, the former is only a relative term, and I will not quarrel with it; they are young compared with Methuselah. For their activity I can vouch. Two brothers have recently passed away. One died in Australia, and the other about twelve months ago at Whiteworks. This was the younger; he was only 84 years of age.

Some members of the Eden family yet remain. Jeffery Eden lived at Fox Tor Farm in its early days; it is said to have been built about 1812. The description given of the house by Eden Phillpotts in his novel " The American Prisoner," though fanciful, is probably not so very wide of the mark. It was built for a gentleman's residence, and Mrs Mortimer, just mentioned, remembers the stables there, which were beautifully paved. Richard Eden, or as he was familiarly called, Dick Eden, for many years a moorman of the south quarter of the Forest, was the son of Jeffery, and was born at Fox Tor about 1824. One of his sisters, who was also born there, is now living at Princetown, and another relative lives at Whiteworks.

A well-known figure at Princetown is Emmanuel Angel, the present sexton, whose father, James Angel, died in 1887 at the age of 94. He, too, was sexton and filled that office for forty years, having acted as assistant to his predecessor, John Curton, who was somewhere about 90 when he died. James Angel at one time resided at Crockern Cottage, where he and his wife used to attend to the wants of the clergymen who came to officiate at Princetown Church. At one time James Angel worked at Tor Royal, where also another Princetown worthy laboured, much of his time being given to the planting of trees. This was Nathaniel Tremills, who presented the late Prince Consort with a dish of trout when his Royal Highness visited Princetown, in 1852. I have mentioned this circumstance in another place (" Hundred Years on Dartmoor"), but gave the name as Mill as furnished

The Ockery, built on the banks of the Blackabrook. It is claimed that two French officers lived here during their parole.

to me, and I am glad to have this opportunity of correcting the mistake.

Descendants of Hugh Hill, who in 1813 was living at Rundle Stone, and of the Floods another old family, are still to be found there. Reference has been made to the Ockery, as the house on the Blackabrook near the Two Bridges road is called. I think that there can be little doubt that Tyrwhitt was the builder of the house.

In 1812 Tyrwhitt was appointed Gentleman-Usher of the Black Rod, and in accordance with custom received the honour of knighthood.

– Chapter Five –

CLOUDS

The 2nd January, 1814, marked an important event in the history of the little town in the Forest. On that day, as an entry in the register shows, a church was opened, the officiating minister being the Rev. J. H. Mason. It was built by the French prisoners, but the interior work was executed by the Americans. Its more immediate purpose was apparently to serve the needs of those connected with the prison and barracks, although sufficient accommodation was afforded for all who had settled in the neighbourhood. In the entry referred to it is not called Princetown Church, but Dartmoor Church, and later on, more correctly, Dartmoor Chapel. At that time, and for many years afterwards, Princetown consisted only of the houses on the Plymouth and Two Bridges roads, and did not extend, as at present, northward towards the prison. It was the latter to which the attention of men was drawn, and not to the little place where butchers and bakers and brewers lived. The prison was Dartmoor Prison, as it is today, and by many off the Moor the name of Princetown was not heard. In a pamphlet on the railway, dated January 1st, 1819, it is Dartmoor that is spoken of all through; Princetown is shown on an accompanying plan, but although the pamphlet was written by Tyrwhitt that place is only mentioned once. On a bill giving notice of a sale by auction of the manor of Gidleigh in 1814, which was kindly lent me by Mr. A. Guy Whipham, the present owner, Gidleigh is described as being ten miles from the New Prison on Dartmoor, plainly indicating that this name was better known than that of Princetown. Miss Sophie Dixon, who lived at Princetown, yet dates the preface of her "Castalian Hours," published in 1828, from Dartmoor, and on a plan and a map, published in 1830, roads are shown as running to Dartmoor Prison, Princetown not being named.

It was nearly two years after the opening of the church before burials took place there. On the first page of the burial register is the following:– "Dartmoor Chapel and Burying Ground: Faculty granted for the interment

The Church of St. Michael and All Angels before it underwent alterations.

of the dead. Novr. 1, 1815."

The first entry occurs eighteen days later:–

"Novr. 19. William Shillingford, Dartmoor Barracks: by minister of Dartmoor Chapel, Rev. J. H. Mason."

Two other entries of those early years are of more than ordinary interest, as apparently relating to the father and aunt of the minister:–

"May 7, 1819. John Mason, Gent., Crockern Tor Cottage, aged 74: performed by Rev. G. H. Hames, Rector of Chagford."

"January 8, 1821. Mary Mason, Spinster (sister of the above), Crockern Tor Cottage, 88 years: performed by Rev. J. Nosworthy, curate of Widecombe."

The Church of St. Michael and All Angels, after the roof had been lowered and the building extended.

It had been the custom to bury the prisoners of war in an enclosure on the eastern side of the prison, and this was not departed from on the opening of the graveyard. The interments seem to have been performed in a careless manner, many of the remains being visible in after years. They were collected in 1865 by Captain W. J. Stopford, Governor of the convict prison, and reinterred in two separate cemeteries formed by him for the purpose on part of the site of the original burying ground. An obelisk was erected in each–one to the memory of the French prisoners, and the other to the memory of the Americans. They are precisely alike, and the inscription setting forth their purpose terminates in each case with the words "Dulce et decorum est pro patria mori." According to a statement of Captain Vernon Harris, who was Governor of the prison about 1880, an acknowledgment of this kind and thoughtful act was received from France, showing that it was duly appreciated in that country. Convicts are buried in the Princetown graveyard.

The church is dedicated to St. Michael and All Angels, and though wanting in the charm of antiquity, and exhibiting no striking features, yet possesses much interest; a melancholy one, it may be but the deeper and stronger for that. It is impossible to look upon its walls, or to mark from afar its storm-beaten tower, without thinking of its builders. How forcibly must the work to which they were putting their hands have reminded them that though of another nation and deprived of freedom, they and their captors were yet brothers. Every stone they placed in the temple told them they were of one faith, the children of one God.

It has been stated that the pulpit was formerly in St. Sidwell's Church at Exeter, but on what grounds does not appear. The bells that were intended to fling "their summons glad" over the heath now hang near the waters. Ere they could be brought to the moorland town men's hearts were gladdened at the tidings of peace. The great prison would soon open its doors, the barracks would be deserted; so another place than Dartmoor Chapel was found for them. They were taken from Plymouth to the Dockyard, and are now hanging in the chapel there.

About the same time as the church was built a row of houses was also erected near by. It stands on the left of the road leading towards the prison, and is now known as Government Row, but formerly bore the name of Church Row, and is frequently mentioned in the registers from 1815 onwards.

A little over six years after the opening of Dartmoor prison of war the need for it no longer existed. England had sheathed the sword, and those she had held captive returned to their own countries. The French prisoners were released in the summer of 1814, but hostilities with America continuing it was not until the 19th April, 1815, that the first draft of men of that nation left the prison. A foul blot stains the history of its latter days. On the evening of the 6th April the Governor, Captain Shortland, discovered a hole in a wall which separated two yards, and supposing that an attempt at escape was on foot ordered an alarm to be sounded. The prisoners rushed out of the various buildings to ascertain the reason of it, and by some means forced open the inner gate. Shortland drew up his soldiers in a position to charge, and the order to fire was given. The prisoners ran towards the doors of the buildings from which they had issued, and while struggling to get within were fired upon. According to an account of the disturbance, written by Charles Andrews, one of the captives, and printed in New York in 1852, the soldiers then advanced and fired another volley, after which, with Shortland at their head, they searched the yard for stray prisoners, deliberately shooting one poor wretch who had been unable to get inside with his companions. Shortland's cruelty and cowardice is altogether inexcusable. He appears to have stood in actual fear of the prisoners, notwithstanding that he was in command of a strong body of soldiery. Seven prisoners were killed and fifty-six wounded. Poor captives who were eagerly

The row of houses on the right is Church Row, later to be called Government Row. Inside one of these, Dissenting services were once held.

looking forward to regain their liberty in a few days ruthlessly shot down. A black page in the annals of Dartmoor; one to make Englishmen sad.

When the prisoners had departed, and the guards were withdrawn, and those who had ministered to their wants had left the scene of their labours, the little town outside the southern boundary gate sank into the old sleepy state that characterised the hamlet out of which it sprung. Clouds obscured the sky; the promise of the morning was not fulfilled; the once busy place lay silent in the cold grey light of the day that had not long broken. Empty dwellings on one hand, and a huge deserted prison and untenanted barracks on the other; signs everywhere of what the brief past had been, but none that spoke of hope to the future.

Among those whom the change in the fortunes of Princetown affected, none perhaps felt the reverse more keenly than Sir Thomas Tyrwhitt. Believing as he did in the possibility of colonising Dartmoor, there is no doubt that he looked upon the town that had been called into existence as an important factor in such a scheme. Its formation was a step towards the realisation of that upon which he had set his mind; by bringing people to the Moor he hoped that they would see in it a land of promise, as he himself did. The decline of the town when the prison was closed showed him that those who had been employed there were far from being convinced that a livelihood was to be gained in such a place. They had learned what the Moor was, and were not impressed by the prospects it offered. But the master of Tor Royal seems to have been a man with whom hope was ever in the ascendant. A town had arisen in the midst of the waste, and though the greater number of its inhabitants had left it, its empty houses might again be occupied if employment could be found for the people. At that time the only buildings northward of that which is now the Duchy Hotel were the church, the parsonage, the bakery, Church Row, the barracks, and the prison. But it is hardly probable that Tyrwhitt contemplated the linking up of these with the little town. It was not extension that he had immediately in view, but the peopling of the partly deserted settlement, and as a matter of fact no additions were made to it until long after his death.

Sir Thomas's great object was to open up Dartmoor, and create what he called a back-country for Plymouth; to turn a vast stretch of wild moor into a productive district. This he saw could not be effected unless an easy means of transit between the two was provided, and thus he was led to suggest the formation of a tram-road. I have before me in the pamphlet already alluded to (and which bears Sir Thomas's autograph), containing the substance of a statement on the subject made by him to the Plymouth Chamber of Commerce on the 3rd November, 1818. In it he sets forth the advantages to be derived from such a road and gives a rosy picture of the capabilities of Dartmoor. The scheme was adopted, and the people in the little lonely town away on the hills saw a few faint beams struggling through the leaden firmament. A few years later the line was completed, its opening being celebrated by a breakfast at the wharf near the present Rock Hotel, on Roborough Down, and a dinner at the Royal Hotel, Plymouth. Then the beams began to drive the clouds away.

– Chapter Six –

DARKER CLOUDS

Present-day company promoters are no way in advance of Sir Thomas Tyrwhitt in their ability to exhibit their projects in the most favourable light. Nothing more enticing than the statements contained in his pamphlet on the proposed railway could well be imagined. Its formation, it is said, would clothe Dartmoor with grain and grasses, and fill it with a hardy population; it would also be the means of providing employment for the poor, and would alleviate the pressure of parochial burdens. And not only was the moorland district to be benefited, but other parts of Devon as well, including the port of Plymouth. The income from the line would be derived chiefly from the tonnage of various commodities which are named under the heads of "Importable" and "Exportable." Among the first are mentioned lime, sea sand, timber, bricks, slate, tiles, laths, coal, culm, groceries, wine, beer, furniture, and trees for planting; and among the second, granite, peat, mining products, flax, and hemp. The scheme would not only "dilate the benevolent heart of the patriot," but there would be the "growing certainties of ulterior advantage," experience having proved that in Scotland railroads had paid dividends of eighteen per cent.

The railroad, which was of course worked by horse power, terminated at Princetown at a yard situated in the rear of the Railway Inn. This was surrounded by a high wall, and was known as the wharf, but it does not appear to have been very long in use. The Moor still failed to attract inhabitants, and early in the history of the line it is probable that Sir Thomas perceived it was not likely to do so much for the district as had been expected. This must have proved a great disappointment, for he had been sanguine of the success of the undertaking, described at that time as a magnificent one. The cornice round the entrance hall at Tor Royal, representing a railway with open trucks, and which is still in excellent preservation, is indicative of the direction in which his thoughts were tending. The day of a quicker mode of transit than that hitherto employed had arrived, and he recognised it. He saw that such was indispensable to the development of any place, and therefore his first care must be to render Dartmoor readily accessible. His ideas about cultivating it may have been wrong– there is little doubt they were – but holding the opinion on the subject which he did he certainly took the right step in bringing forward his scheme. Still, his railway was not to re-people Princetown; the gleams of light that at first were so promising were obscured. It was but a temporary break in the clouds, and when they gathered again they looked more threatening than before.

The chief use to which the Plymouth and Dartmoor railroad was put was not to convey the numerous commodities named in Sir Thomas's pamphlet, but the carriage of granite from the Foggin Tor Quarries. The hoped-for building, and planting, and flax growing never took place. Besides quarrymen few fresh residents came into the neighbourhood, and many of those lived at or near, Rundle Stone, and not at Princetown. This industry, however, was to prove beneficial to the little town later on, and thus indirectly it was served by the railroad. But it did not bring the settler to the Moor: the man who was to create the farms of which Sir Thomas dreamed; it did not revive the fallen fortunes of Princetown. Notwithstanding that he sought by every means to promote the welfare of the latter, among other things procuring for it the privilege of holding a market and a fair; six years after the railroad was opened, namely, in 1828, the place is described by Henry Carrington, son of the poet, as " a collection of about half a dozen miserable hovels and two good inns, chiefly supported by travellers traversing the Moor from Moreton to Plymouth and Devonport." And Sir Thomas Tyrwhitt did not live to see it rise out of this slough, which, however, was not exactly that of Despond, for the quarries gave some hopes of a revival of its fortunes. Sir Thomas died in February, 1833, as is set forth on a tablet in Princetown Church. The inscription states truly that "his name and memory are inseparable from all the great works in Dartmoor"; but while this is so there will be many who will wish that he had never made it a field of operations. The Nature lover certainly has no reason to rejoice at his work, and that he was the cause, directly and indirectly, of much land being taken from the commoner is equally true. But he was a man whom it is impossible not to admire. He thoroughly believed in his undertakings on the Moor, and proved his unselfishness in investing large sums of money in projects which it was only too evident could not yield a return speedily enough to benefit him. He thought he could conquer Dartmoor, or at least point the way by which it might be done, and though he failed his indomitable perseverance is none the less deserving of our praise.

The quarries at Foggin Tor were at first worked by the Messrs. Johnsons

Prison officers standing opposite Church or Government Row.

and Brice of London, who held an assignment of a long lease of the granite on Walkhampton Common, granted by Sir Masseh Lopes to the railway company. They were afterwards worked by the Messrs. Freeman, a name well known at the present day in connection with the granite industry in Cornwall. It is said that when the quarries were in full work as many as 600 men were employed there, and though by far the greater number of these lived outside Princetown, the little place at such times showed some slight reflection of its old aspect. Both Mr. James Rowe and, afterwards, his son, Mr. James Julian Rowe, felt the benefit of the industry, their forges often presenting a busy scene. One good dame, who lived at Two Bridges, did a thriving trade at that time. She was known as Granny Jenkins, and kept a shop, which was situated just opposite to the present Two Bridges Hotel, from which she supplied Princetown with large quantities of eggs, butter, and other produce, gathered from the Post Bridge neighbourhood.

It was during the busier days of the quarries that Dissenting services were first held at Princetown, a room in a house in Church Row, occupied by Samuel Vinnycombe, a Wesleyan, and a stonemason at Foggin Tor, being used for the purpose. He conducted the services himself, and was known as a most devout, peaceful, and God-fearing man. Later on the services were held in a larger room in the house over the shop now kept by Mr. Bolt, and subsequently a small chapel was built, chiefly through the instrumentality of the late Mr. Duke who was the principal force in the building of the present Wesleyan Chapel, which stands near to the entrance to Tor Royal. A chapèl and school were also opened at Foggin Tor about fifty years ago.

After Sir Thomas Tyrwhitt's death, in 1833, Tor Royal was occupied by a Mr. Nicholson, who restarted the mine at Bachelor's Hall, which, it is said, produced good tin. One of those connected with it was in his time a prominent figure in this part of the Moor. This was Captain Billy Mitchell, who came from Lanteglos, and now lies buried in Princetown graveyard. In 1844 Tor Royal was sold to Mr. James Cholmondely Russell, who is remembered by the older inhabitants as "Mr. Chimley." He lived there for about three years, and there was a large sale of farm stock when he left. Later in the century Tor Royal became the home of the late Mr. Charles Barrington, High Bailiff of Dartmoor, and is at present in the occupation of his son, Mr. A. E. Barrington, who has succeeded to that position.

Several enterprises were started at and near Princetown in the years following Sir Thomas Tyrwhitt's death, but none of them can be said to have proved successful. About 1844 works for the extraction of naphtha from peat were commenced at Bachelor's Hall, and were afterwards

Crockern Farm where naphtha was once extracted from peat.

removed to the unoccupied war prison, and there were also similar works, but on a smaller scale, at Crockern Farm. Many people were employed in cutting peat, at first in Tor Royal Newtake, and afterwards on Holming Beam. A tramroad was constructed from the latter place to the works at the prison, for the conveyance of the peat. The manager of these large works was Mr. Stocker (not Stockman, as stated in my "Hundred Years"), and with him were associated several well-known Plymothians of that day.

But these efforts to bring prosperity once more to Princetown were of little avail; Dartmoor's back may be scratched, but unlike the dog, he will resent it, and punish you for your pains. The following words, written about this time, give us a picture of Princetown as it then was: "The deserted village of Princetown . . . with its falling houses, its closed inn, its mean-looking church . . . and churchyard waving with rank grass and tall nettles. . . . It seemed an unhonoured and unfrequented spot. Never did I behold a scene of more utter desolation."

A few years, and this was to be changed. In November, 1850 a party of 200 prisoners arrived, for the purpose of making the alterations necessary to render the prison suitable for the reception of convicts.

✣ ✣ ✣

– Chapter Seven –

A CLEARER SKY

A proposal to utilise the war prison as a prison for convicts had been made soon after the conclusion of peace, as is shown by a Report of a Committee of the House of Commons on the Prisons of the Metropolis; an extract from which is given by Sir Thomas Tyrwhitt in his pamphlet on the railway. But as we have seen this was not then carried into effect; nor was another scheme, put forth in 1820, to use the building as a home in which the child waifs of the streets of London might receive moral and industrial training. It was only when towards the middle of the 19th century it was recognised that the huge building did not adapt itself to private enterprise that the Government again took it in hand, the suggestion put forth more than thirty years before by the Parliamentary Committee having been revived. This was after a visit to Princetown by the Prince Consort, in 1846, and it has been said that it was largely upon his advice that the former scheme was reverted to.

With the establishment of the convict prison trade in Princetown began to revive. The clouds that had so long hung over the little place were dispelled: the blue became visible, the bright sun showed his face. The hopes of the people ran high – there was promise of work for their hands to do. Those who remembered the town in the time of war looked with confidence to a return of those busy days. Their expectations were justified; the light that then shone upon Princetown has never been obscured.

In 1850 Mr. James Rowe was still at the Railway Inn, but Perry's Directory of that year speaks of the building known as the Duchy Hotel as being empty. It was however, taken about that time by Mr. James Julian Rowe, who had for some time resided in Church Row, where the present Mr. Aaron Rowe was born. When he took possession the house was in a sad state of decay; moss covered the walls of the rooms in places and the plant that follows man wherever he goes – the nettle – on the floors; but in his hands it speedily became the foremost hostelry on Dartmoor. I have heard

The gateways to Dartmoor Prison, the outer one bearing the motto "Parcere Subjectis". This photograph was taken prior to 1901, as can be seen by the letters V and R on the "NOTICE" board.

The Courtyard at Dartmoor Prison showing the convicts taking exercise.

The Duchy Hotel before it was restored in 1908.

The Interior of the Duchy Hotel.

on very good authority that the Prince Consort was a visitor at the hotel in 1846, but I do not see how this can be as I cannot learn that it was a house of entertainment before Mr. Rowe took it, and it was for many years in the condition described above. I think it must have been in 1852 that the Prince Consort stayed there, as he came again to Princetown in that year to inspect the convict prison. Another hostelry was opened about this time. This was the Albert Hotel, now called the Imperial Hotel, so that the Plume of Feathers, the once lonely roadside inn, saw within less than half a century three rivals grow up near it. Later on when more houses were built, a forth appeared, the Prince of Wales Hotel.Soon after the prison was opened evidences of the changed state of things were everywhere observable. Mr Rowe having contracted to supply the ironwork required at the prison, his forges again presented a scene of animation, and this continued until the authorities took that class of work into their own hands. There was continual going and coming; wagons were no longer a rarity on the Dartmoor roads. The railway brought some few of the commodities mentioned by Sir Thomas Tyrwhitt as "Importable," flour being one of them. This was supplied by Mr. Ellis, of Plymouth, and was conveyed over the line in a covered van constructed for the purpose. Meat does not appear to have been carried over it, possibly because the purveyors at Plymouth regarded the sending of such to a district where cattle and sheep were numerous as being akin to taking coals to Newcastle. If so, they laboured under a mistake. Meat had to be " imported," but it was left for Lydford to supply it. It was brought from that place by a Mr. Gill, but seems to have been something of a luxury, his stall, which adjoined the tollhouse opposite the Plume of Feathers, being only open on Saturdays. He continued to serve his customers until about forty years since, when greater facilities were established. An industry was also started in 1852. William Babb, having discovered a bed of clay (it may seen about midway between the Duchy Hotel and the railway station), built some kilns on the north side of the Plymouth road, and commenced the making of bricks. But the venture proved unsuccessful, and the buildings he erected were converted into dwellings. These which have been before referred to are known as Babb's Cottages. Near the site of the clay-bed was the first telegraph office at Princetown, which was known locally as Noah's Ark.

The Rev. Rook Fletcher was in charge of Princetown Church, or of the Chapel-of-Ease, as it was termed in 1850. At present the Rev. Henry Knowles has charge of it. The rector is the Rev. G. S. Thorpe, who resides at Lydford.

When the alterations at the prison were effected, cells for the convicts were constructed in each of the large buildings grouped around the inner space. These cells were of corrugated iron, and were placed in a line down the centre of the buildings, so that the officers on duty paraded between them and the walls. This arrangement was continued for about twenty years, when a large prison, known as No. 5, was built. This was followed by another, No. 4c, and a part of the old prisons previously used was then converted into storerooms and workshops. Later on in 1885, another block was opened, No. 2c, and shortly afterwards basket-making was introduced, and was carried on for many years in the old No. 3 prison. About 1890 a large shed was erected for the manufacture of twine, and subsequently a commodious carpenters' shop, with steam circular saw and other appliances, was built. Extensive additions to the tailoring and shoemaking departments were also made, as well as improvements in the heating arrangements throughout the prison; and also in the Protestants and Roman Catholic chapels and the hospital. In 1901 a substantial block of sixty cells was opened, intended chiefly for prisoners undergoing dietary punishment, and for those about to be released. This new building also contains an adjunction room for the use of the Board of Visiting Justices, who attend at the prison on the first Wednesday in each month. In 1905 another block was opened, built mostly of concrete, and it is now computed that about eight hundred modern cells have been added to this prison since 1851, each cell costing about £100. Outside the boundary wall of the prison there were formerly seven guardhouses, but these together with about a dozen other houses situated within the barracks, were condemned as insanitary by Mr. W. S. Frew, the chief medical officer of the prison from 1884 to 1903, and were consequently demolished. Additional quarters have however, been built for the officers engaged at the prison, and these form an important addition to the moorland town. There are sixty of them, the buildings being known locally as Garsia-terrace, but at the Home-office they figure as A, B, C, and D, Blocks.

The first Governor of the convict prison was Captain Gambier; the present Governor is Mr. Basil Thomson. In the early days soldiers were quartered at the barracks. Three poor fellows belonging to this force lost their lives in the snowstorm on the Moor in February 1853. The 7th Royal Fusiliers were at that time stationed at Princetown, and two of the unfortunate men were on their way to join their company there, the other being a corporal who had gone on the road to meet them. There is a tablet to their memory in Princetown Church. Now a body of men known as the Civil Guard keep watch and ward over the prisoners. Soon after the opening of the convict prison the houses on either side of the road northward of the Duchy Hotel were commenced to be built, and additions to the place were also made in the Two Bridges road. Another was made

An aerial view of the convict prison.

The road to Two Bridges looking towards New London on the skyline. On the left is Bolt's Store and on the right the Tea Rooms and Boarding House owned by W. Bowden. It is now the Fox Tor Cafe.

Princetown Railway Station.

The Dartmoor "Express".

about 1873. This consisted of some houses erected originally as dwellings for the men employed at Whiteworks, but about the time they were completed the mine ceased working, so that they were not required for that purpose. They are known as New London in consequence of the architect, contractors, and clerk of the works all belonging to the metropolis. A second glance is not needed to convince anyone that no Dartmoor man had a hand in designing them; those who are acquainted with that region know that high houses are not there desirable. They stand near the Two Bridges road, and form a conspicuous landmark from the Moreton road beyond Post Bridge.

Among objects in and around Princetown to which old memories cling may be named a track made by the war prisoners, and known as Frenchmen's Road; and also the building called the Ockery, in, or near to, which one, or perhaps two, prisoners according to stories formerly related, and for which there appears to be good ground, were once confined.

One of the most important events in the history of Princetown was the construction of the railway, which was formed almost throughout its whole length on the line of Sir Thomas Tyrwhitt's old tramroad. It did not come until nearly fifty years after Sir Thomas's death, but that he saw it in imagination is not to be doubted. The open wagons figured on the cornice at Tor Royal, before referred to, are represented as being drawn by Stephenson's first locomotive.

Princetown and Two Bridges entered with zest into the Jubilee rejoicings in 1887 and 1897. In commemoration of the first event a lamp was erected by public subscription in the centre of the open space in front of the Duchy Hotel. It stands on the spot formerly occupied by the tollhouse.

In July, 1903 their Royal Highnesses the Prince and Princess of Wales visited Princetown. The occasion is a memorable one, this being the first time that a Lord of Dartmoor had entered his Forest for many years. The Royal party crossed the Moor in two motor cars, Mr. A. E. Barrington accompanying the one in which the Prince and Princess rode.

And now we will bid the little town in the wilderness good-bye – but let us hope, not finally. Though yet young it will be admitted that it is not altogether wanting in interest. Born at a time when the thoughts of Englishmen were directed to the battlefield, its early years knew only bustle and turmoil; every sound and every sight spoke of war. Since then it has witnessed alternate periods of prosperity and decay. That it should have had its struggles with adversity is meet. That which arrives at maturity quickly seldom lives long. Checks to progress are sometimes salutary. But the gloom that so often rested upon Princetown has vanished, and though some of us may regret that the primeval solitude of the Moor should have been intruded upon, we cannot now wish other than that the clouds shall never gather over it again, and that its sun, that rose in the days of the master of Tor Royal, shall never set.

On the left of this street is the old Police Station while on the extreme right is the Imperial Hotel. From where the convicts are coming out is now Bellever Close.

A street scene showing a GWR wagon outside the Princetown and District Co-operative Store.

Duchy Square, with Bolt's Store on the left and the Railway Hotel on the right.

Index